NIGHT CREATURES

GALLERY BOOKS
An Imprint of W. H. Smith Publishers Inc.
112 Madison Avenue
New York City 10016

This edition first published in U.S.
in 1991 by Gallery Books,
an imprint of W.H. Smith Publishers, Inc.
112 Madison Avenue, New York, New York 10016

ISBN 0-8317-9569-7

Printed and bound in Spain

For rights information about the photographs in
this book please contact:

The Image Bank
111 Fifth Avenue, New York, NY 10003

In memory of David R. Hunter

Producer: Solomon M. Skolnick
Writer: Barbara Nielsen
Design Concept: Lesley Ehlers
Designer: Ann-Louise Lipman
Editor: Sara Colacurto
Production: Valerie Zars
Photo Researcher: Edward Douglas
Assistant Photo Researcher: Robert V. Hale
Editorial Assistant: Carol Raguso

Title page: Bathed in moonlight, an Indian fruit bat, *Pteropus giganteus,* extends its membranous wings. By feeding at night, it avoids competition from fruit-eating birds. *Opposite:* The enormous eyes of the long-eared owl, *Asio otus,* are adapted for hunting at night. Their light-gathering ability is estimated to be two-and-a-half times greater than that of humans.

The mournful howling of wolves, the hooting of owls, the eerie scream of a panther – the sounds of the night have long sent shivers through humankind. As creatures of the day, we have come to associate darkness with death and evil. Yet for a surprising number of life forms, including most mammals, "the dead of night" is very much alive.

Each day, as the sun sets and diurnal animals retreat to their burrows, caves, or electrically lit houses, night creatures venture out from their hiding places. Under cover of darkness, they feed, find mates, and defend their territories; they remain alert for predators and care for their young.

Animals that are mainly active at night have chosen the darkness for various reasons. In some cases, it is the best time for them to hunt or to avoid predators. Other creatures adapt to the night to exploit a niche already taken by day. Thus an owl assumes the role of the diurnal hawk, bats take over where birds leave off, and moths emerge when butterflies have retired.

Specialized environments also influence behavior. Many desert dwellers escape the heat by confining their activity to the cool of night, while cave dwellers and burrowing animals adapt to the black world found underground. At the earth's poles, wildlife adjusts to alternating seasons of night and day.

Clutching a meal for its chicks, a barn owl, *Tyto alba,* approaches its nest in a bell tower. Mice, frogs, and other small prey make up the bulk of its diet.

The barn owl's mottled feathers are an effective camouflage by day. During courtship, owls rely on vocal displays rather than colorful plumage to attract potential mates. *Below:* The soundless flight of a barn owl allows it to swoop undetected on its prey. Muffled wing-beats have a second advantage: they don't interfere with the owl's hearing.

The saw-whet owl, *Aegolius acadicus*, is rarely seen by day. At night, its whistling call can be heard in North American deciduous forests. *Below:* The nightjar, genus *Caprimulgus*, swoops up from its hiding place to take insects on the wing. Roughly 70 species of nightjars, including the American whip-poor-will and the Australian frogmouth, are found around the world.

Preceding pages, left: The boreal owl, *Aegolius funereus,* a relative of the saw-whet, populates coniferous forests throughout Canada. *Right:* Male and female screech owls, *Otus asio,* trill back and forth to each other in eerie nocturnal duets. These vocalizations are part of the mating ritual. *This page:* A sleepy-looking great horned owl, *Bubo virginianus,* snuggles close to its downy chick. In the months to come, the owlet will acquire essential night-hunting skills.

The nightingale, *Luscinia megarynchos*, uses its melodious song to mark the borders of its territory. *Below:* New Zealand's brown kiwi, *Apteryx australis*, is a flightless forest dweller. This near-sighted bird detects its earthworm prey by sniffing the soil with its long bill. *Opposite:* Amphibians such as this leopard frog, *Rana pipiens*, avoid the drying effects of the sun by adopting a night-active lifestyle.

To successfully navigate in the darkness, animals have fine-tuned one or more of the senses. The huge, rounded eyes characteristic of many night creatures are designed to take advantage of low levels of light. Many animals enhance this light-gathering ability with the aid of a tapetum, or mirrorlike surface, behind the retina, which reflects light back through the eye. The tapetum is responsible for the glow seen when a flashlight beam shines on the face of a nocturnal creature such as a cat. During the day, the animal's light-sensitive eyes are protected by pupils that shrink to a narrow slit.

Night vision is also improved by a retina packed with rods. Generally speaking, rods enable an animal to see in dim light, while cones provide sharpness and color vision. Most nocturnal animals have few, if any, cones; they see a rather fuzzy picture and view the world in shades of black and white. They use their eyes to detect movement and basic shapes and rely on other senses for help in interpreting these data.

For many night creatures, hearing plays an important role, especially on a black, moonless night, when even the best nocturnal vision is useless. The large outer ears of many night-active animals — including rabbits, the fennec fox, and the aardwolf — funnel even the slightest rustle to the inner ear, helping them avoid predators or

The high-pitched call of the Pacific treefrog, *Hyla regilla*, is a common sound along the West Coast. Frogs rely on their distinctive vocalizations to communicate in the darkness. *Below:* Swelled to nearly bursting, a barking treefrog, *Hyla gratiosa*, calls from a South Carolina swamp. This species has two distinct calls: the breeding call, a bell-like sound, and the more common bark. *Opposite:* A red-eyed treefrog from Coast Rica, *Agalychnis callidryas*, has enlarged orbs for better night vision.

locate prey. The insect-eating aardvark has such acute hearing that it can detect the faint sound of a column of ants on the move.

The ability to hear well is important for another reason. Loud vocalizations – croaks, screams, booms, chatters, yips, and yowls – are used by night creatures to announce the borders of their territory and to find mates. This is why the night is often so noisy, especially during mating season, when insects, frogs, and roaring alligators advertise their presence to potential partners.

Many nocturnal animals also have a keen sense of smell. As with the other senses, it is used in avoiding predators or in tracking down prey, a mate, or an intruder.

Closely related to smell is taste. This is especially important to reptiles and amphibians, who use their Jacobsen's organs – sensory devices that allow them to "smell the food in the mouth" – to determine whether prey is edible.

The final sense is that of touch, which can assume paramount importance in a world dimly seen. The sensitive whiskers of cats, otters, and other animals help guide them in the darkness, while the long-fingered raccoon relies on its sense of touch when probing for crawfish and minnows in streambeds. Tree-dwelling mammals such as the slow loris feel their way along branches with a methodical, hand-over-hand grip; burrowing moles process information with their tactile snouts.

This page: **A startled bullfrog,** *Rana catesbeiana,* **leaps to the safety of a pond. Its bulbous eyes are alert to moving objects, and it quickly reacts to anything large.**

Once in the water, the bullfrog propels itself forward with its powerful legs and webbed hind feet.

A female loggerhead turtle, *Caretta caretta*, drags herself up a Florida beach under cover of darkness. Using her hind flippers, she digs a deep nest in the sand, fills it with eggs, and covers them before heading back to sea. *Below:* After weeks of incubation in the sun, the eggs hatch. Hatchlings follow the shimmer of starlight on the ocean to reach the surf.

Nature's night life probably began some 350 million years ago, when the ancestors of the amphibians crept out from the sea and began adapting to life on land. They evolved primitive lungs, but found it necessary to supplement their oxygen supply by breathing through their moist skins. Thus, the vast majority of amphibians are nocturnal, an adaption that lets them avoid the drying effects of the sun. By day, they hide in a cool, dark place – under a log or stone, or in the shade of shoreline vegetation – and emerge at dusk to feed.

Amphibians are well adapted for moving about at night. Most have excellent hearing, which not only helps them avoid predators but is also useful in locating mates. Frogs are among the most vocal of the night creatures. Females are able to find males in the dark by pinpointing the source of the grunt, croak, peep, or bark. The distinctive voice of each species helps

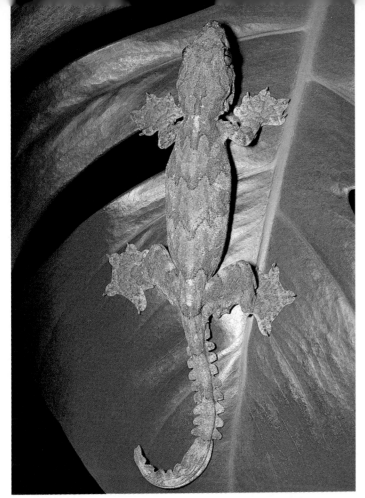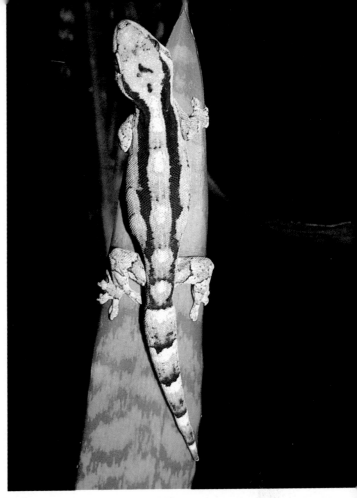

Above, left to right: **The flying gecko,** *Ptychozoon kuhli,* **is capable of making prodigious leaps; its fall is slowed by folds of skin on its sides that billow out like parachutes. The Wahlberg's gecko,** *Homopholis wahlbergi,* **has large eyes that function well in low levels of light.**
Below: **The zigzagging pupil of the Tokay gecko,** *Gekko gecko,* **shrinks by day to protect the reptile's light-sensitive retina. Grit is cleaned from its eye with a quick swipe of the tongue.**

prevent cases of mistaken identity; during mating season, the din can be deafening as individual frogs turn up the volume to make themselves heard.

The peculiar, bulging eyes of many toads and frogs allow them to see forward, backward, to the sides, and up. Though their vision is generally myopic, they react quickly to movement, flicking out a long, sticky tongue to snare a passing insect or hurriedly hopping away from anything large.

Because most amphibians snap up any moving, insect-sized object they encounter, they rely on their sense of smell to determine whether the prey is edible. The analysis is made with their Jacobsen's organs. Inedible items are immediately spat out, while savory insects are swallowed. Interestingly, the frog's bulbous eyes assist it in eating. As the frog swallows, its eyes are depressed, thus forcing the food down the gullet.

Reptiles were able to break their ties with the water by developing better lungs and encasing their eggs in shells. As they no longer needed the thin, damp skins of their amphibian ancestors, they evolved tough, scaly coverings that provided better protection.

Above: **The deadly black widow spider,** *Latrodectus mactans,* **avoids the sun. Insects are trapped at night in its well-placed web, then killed with its potent venom.** *Left:* **The wolf spider,** *Geolycosa,* **takes its name from its habit of chasing down its prey. Its keen eyes detect the slightest movements.** *Opposite:* **Now that dawn has arrived, this black-and-yellow spider,** *Argiope aurantia,* **will retreat from view to avoid predatory birds.**

A lone firefly, *Pterophyx malaccae*, signals to a potential mate in the dark of a summer night. Each species has its own distinct pattern of flashes. *Below:* Thousands of male fireflies gather in a mangrove bush in Singapore to flash *en masse*. This phenomenon occurs only in Asia.

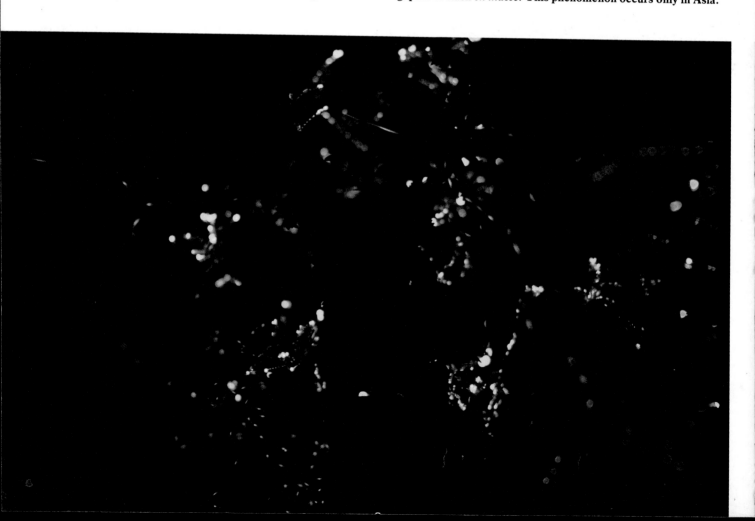

Above: The delicately patterned polyphemus moth, *Antheraea polyphemus,* has eyespots on its wings designed to frighten predators. *Below, left to right:* Like most moths, the promethea, *Callosamia promethia,* does not rely on visual cues in finding a mate; females attract males by secreting a chemical pheromone that can be detected several miles away. The cecropia moth, *Hyalophora cecropia,* lives an average of ten days in its adult form, during which time it does not eat.

Preceding page: The large eyes of the flying squirrel, *Glaucomys volans,* guide its movements as it glides from tree to tree. By adopting a night-active lifestyle, it avoids diurnal predators like hawks. *This page, right:* A stripe-faced dunnart, *Sminthopsis macroura,* ventures out with her young in the cool of the desert night. Many animals avoid the desert sun by foraging after dark. *Below:* A flashlight beam picks up the eye-glow of a South African springhare, *Padetes capensis.* A common feature in nocturnal creatures, shining eyes are the result of the mirror-like tapetum behind the animal's retina.

The European mole, *Talpa europaea*, uses its tactile snout and paws to guide its movements underground. Vision plays no role in its permanently dark world.

A well-known scavenger, the brown rat, *Rattus norvegicus,* scurries about under cover of darkness. The vast majority of rodents are nocturnal. *Below:* Ever alert, a plump meadow vole, *Microtis pennsylvanicus,* nibbles on a strawberry. Voles are preyed upon by owls, coyotes, and other night hunters. *Opposite:* An omnivorous night wanderer, the striped skunk, *Mephitis mephitis,* relies on its obnoxious odor to fend off predators.

A relative of the raccoon, the petit, or lesser, panda, *Ailurus fulgens,* is rarely seen by day. It feeds on leaves, fruit, insects, and occasional eggs. *Below:* The sensitive fingers of the raccoon, *Procyon lotor,* are useful for probing in creek beds after dark. Fish, crawfish, and frogs make up part of its diet.

Reptiles are limited by the fact that they are unable to regulate their body temperature. The vast majority solve this problem by alternately basking in the sun and cooling off in the shade. As a result, most are diurnal. The exceptions are those that live in warm, tropical climates or desert regions. A number of these have chosen a nocturnal lifestyle to take advantage of available prey.

While most reptiles have adequate eyesight, they rely more on their sense of smell when searching for food. A snake's flicking tongue is used to gather scent particles, which are passed back to its Jacobsen's organs; if a smell proves interesting, the snake hones in for the kill.

Sounds also reveal potential prey. Although snakes lack ears, they are able to "hear" ground vibrations through their bodies. The common krait, a deadly night-hunting snake found in India, uses this sense to locate rodents in residential dwellings or along trails; every year, kraits accidentally kill some 15,000 people as they strike out at anything that moves.

Venomous pit vipers, which are mostly nocturnal, have developed a sensitivity to heat that allows them to detect the presence of warm-blooded mammals. These unusual sensory organs appear as small pits underneath the eyes. Rattlesnakes,

Above: **Sharp spines provide an effective defense for the prehensile-tailed porcupine,** *Coendou prehensilis.* **This South American species uses its long tail to assist it in climbing.** *Right:* **Porcupines are found in both the Old and New Worlds. They live on bark, roots, and leaves and confine their foraging to night.**

A porcupine family waddles undisturbed
through the African night. Not even the
lion will approach their bristly silhouettes.

Preceding page: A native of South America, the tamandua anteater, *Tamandua tetradactyla,* uses its long, sticky tongue to probe for ants. *This page, above:* A Cape pangolin, or scaly anteater, *Manis temminckii,* pauses for a drink. A nocturnal forager, the pangolin feeds on ants and termites, which it tracks down with its sensitive nose. *Below:* When in danger, the pangolin curls up in a ball. Its scaly "armor" is an effective defense.

The three-toed sloth, *Bradypus tridactylus*, can hang motionless for hours in its rain-forest home. At night, it swings through the trees, slowly munching leaves, fruit, and flowers. *Below:* The two-toed sloth, *Choloepus didactylus*, is smaller and slightly more active than its three-toed relative. *Opposite:* Sloths rely on their dull coloration to hide them from view by day. In the rainy season, green algae grows in their long hair, making them even harder to spot.

moccasins, and the much-feared fer-de-lance, a tropical snake whose bite results in massive hemorrhaging, all belong to this family.

Very few birds are on the wing at night, probably because they evolved from reptiles and found no reason to switch from daytime activity. The exceptions include owls, nightjars, and such anomalies as the kiwi, an odd, flightless species that emerges at night to sniff for earthworms with its long bill, and the cave-dwelling oil bird, the only nocturnal bird to feed on fruit. Interestingly, the oil bird is equipped with echolocation, which it uses not to locate food but to find its way back to its roost at night. The fruit it dines on has a pungent smell, which makes it easy to find.

Owls are among the most famous of the night creatures. Their enormous eyes absorb all available light, and their night vision is further enhanced by a preponderance of rods as opposed to cones.

An owl's eyes are so large in relation to its head that it lacks the space for muscles with which to move them. Instead, it has the peculiar ability to rotate its head almost completely around, as well as upside down.

This page, top to bottom: **The slender loris of India,** *Loris tardigradus,* **is a primitive primate that feeds exclusively on insects; it has excellent night vision and highly sensitive ears. A relative of the raccoon, the kinkajou,** *Potos flavus,* **is easily identified by its long prehensile tail. The northern quoll,** *Dasyurus hallucatus,* **a marsupial of Australia, is one of four species of native cats; it is extremely agile and hunts at night for insects and other small prey.** *Opposite:* **The lesser bushbaby,** *Galago senegalensis,* **a native of Africa, has such light-sensitive eyes that it can barely function in daylight.**

A pair of Goodfellow tree kangaroos, *Dendrolagus goodfellowi*, feed on rain-forest vegetation in Papua New Guinea. Contrary to popular belief, most kangaroos are nocturnal. *Below:* Australia's spotted cuscus, *Phalanger maculatus*, is adapted to an arboreal life. Like most marsupials, it is active at night.

Above, left to right: **A relative of the raccoon, the nocturnal ringtail cat,** *Bassariscus astutus,* **is also known as the cacomistle, or "cunning cat-squirrel," and has a beautiful black-and-white tail as long as its body. Although both are active at night, Australia's ringtail possum,** *Pseudocheirus herbertensis,* **is not closely related to the American opossum.** *Below:* **The common, or Virginian, opossum,** *Didelphis virginiana,* **is the only marsupial in the United States; by day it hides in a hollow log or dark crevice, emerging at night to rummage about for eggs, fruit, insects, and roots.**

Due to their lack of cones, owls are short-sighted, which is why they hunt close to the ground. Their excellent sense of hearing, however, works in tandem with their vision, allowing them to swoop down accurately on their prey.

Because most birds are inactive at night, bats developed the ability to fly in order to plunder the niches abandoned by the birds after dark. There are a staggering number of species – roughly 950, nearly all of which are nocturnal.

Insect-eating bats are well known for their use of echolocation when hunting at night. They zero in on their prey by emitting bursts of high-frequency sounds and listening for the returning echoes. This technique is also used by the blood-lapping vampire bats of Central and South America and by carnivorous bats that prey on fish, small rodents, and lizards.

Fruit-eating bats rely on their excellent vision and keen sense of smell to lead them to the ripe fruit they feed on. A few species are equipped with a primitive sort of sonar, but it is used mostly for navigation.

By day, most bats hide in the darkness of caves or tree hollows, often in gregarious colonies. The exceptions are a few fruit-eating species that wrap themselves in their dark wings and hang, fully exposed, in trees. Despite their seeming vulnerability, they emit such an obnoxious odor that would-be predators pass them by.

The maruspial sugar glider of Australia, *Petaurus breviceps*, fills the same niche as America's flying squirrel.

The nocturnal koala, *Phascolarctos cinereus*, drowses by day in a eucalyptus tree. Its diet consists of eucalyptus leaves and flowers. *Below:* Baby koalas spend their first six months in their mother's pouch, then cling to her back until they are half-grown. *Opposite:* Nearly eight million koalas were killed in the early 1900's for their fur. Today the species is making a comeback thanks to conservation efforts.

Bats are not the only mammals to work the night shift. Indeed, some biologists believe that the earliest mammals became warm-blooded in order to adopt a nocturnal lifestyle, taking to the cover of darkness to avoid the predatory reptiles that then dominated the earth.

Australia's marsupials bear this theory out. This primitive group of pouch-bearing mammals developed in isolation from the rest of the world, cut off after the Australian continent broke away from the great southern land mass to which it was once connected. Australia's marsupials include the koala, the Tasmanian devil, and many species of wallabies and kangaroos, not to mention marsupial cats, mice, squirrels, and dogs. They are overwhelmingly nocturnal and have developed adaptations to support their activity at night.

By day, the koala clings sleepily to the trunk of the eucalyptus tree, hidden in the vegetation. It awakens at night to munch on the fragrant leaves, guided to its food by its large, sensitive nose.

Kangaroos are also nocturnal, though their fondness for basking in the sun may lead one to assume otherwise. They are herd animals that browse on grasses and are equipped with excellent hearing and a keen sense of smell. When threatened, they bound quickly away.

Preceding pages, left: Seldom seen because of its secretive habits, the Australian tiger cat, *Dasyurus maculatus,* lives in wooded areas. *Right:* The night-active Tasmanian devil, *Sarcophilus harrisi,* has a ferocious reputation, largely due to the fact that it sometimes attacks domestic animals. *These pages:* The Tasmanian devil's powerful teeth make short work of its prey. It eats the entire kill, including bones.

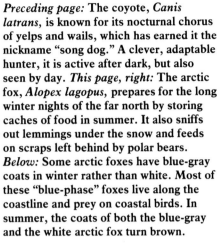

Preceding page: The coyote, *Canis latrans,* is known for its nocturnal chorus of yelps and wails, which has earned it the nickname "song dog." A clever, adaptable hunter, it is active after dark, but also seen by day. *This page, right:* The arctic fox, *Alopex lagopus,* prepares for the long winter nights of the far north by storing caches of food in summer. It also sniffs out lemmings under the snow and feeds on scraps left behind by polar bears. *Below:* Some arctic foxes have blue-gray coats in winter rather than white. Most of these "blue-phase" foxes live along the coastline and prey on coastal birds. In summer, the coats of both the blue-gray and the white arctic fox turn brown.

This page: A spotted, or laughing, hyena, *Crocuta crocuta*, nurses her young on an African plain. Though it was once believed that hyenas were scavengers, they are formidable pack hunters who run down their prey at night. *Opposite:* Hyenas devour nearly every scrap available on a kill, even cracking open bones to get at the marrow.

The most abundant of all mammals are the rodents, which are primarily nocturnal. In addition to the midnight scamperings of rats and mice, porcupines gnaw on bark under cover of darkness, beavers cut down trees, and desert-dwelling gerbils and jerboas forage in the cool of night. Most rabbits are nocturnal, too, and depend on their sensitive ears to warn them of danger.

Other mammals active at night include the insect-eating aardvark, which gathers up termites with its long, sticky tongue; the omnivorous skunk, which rambles about in search of eggs, fruit, insects, and other foods; and the vegetarian sloth, which is surprisingly un-slothful at night, swinging through the trees of a tropical forest in search of tender leaves and flowers.

Also on the prowl at night are the large predators, which either hunt in packs or rely on stealth. Members of the canine family are the ultimate pack hunters, of which wolves and hyenas are prime examples. Both single out a victim from a herd and wear it down with their relentless pursuit. Darkness puts their prey at a disadvantage, which is why most of their hunting is confined to night.

This page, top to bottom: **The white facial markings of the spotted genet,** *Genetta genetta,* **help other genets identify it at night. Like most members of the cat family, the African serval,** *Felis serval,* **is a solitary hunter that is secretive and seldom seen by day. Slight movements are easily detected by the sensitive ears of the swift running caracal,** *Lynx caracal.* *Opposite:* **The ocelot,** *Felis pardalis,* **is difficult to see in the dense forests of South America because of its dappled coat.**

For the same reason, most cats are nocturnal, too, though, with the exception of the lion, they are solitary hunters. They have large, sensitive eyes enhanced by a light-gathering tapetum and ears that are alert to the snap of a twig. The stalkers among them sneak up on their prey, body held low, while ambushers such as leopards crouch in trees and wait for unwary animals to pass underneath.

Large predators are particularly fond of grazing animals, which, for the most part, try to restrict their nocturnal movements in order to avoid detection. But because their food source is inefficient, many herd animals must awaken some-time during the night for an extra meal, while some browse at inter-vals around the clock. Elephants are mostly active by day but enjoy a midnight snack; so do antelopes and zebras, which, unlike the elephant, must remain alert for hungry lions.

Some grazers prefer to feed at night. The heat-sensitive hippo-potamus spends the daylight hours avoiding the sun by submerging itself in water. At night, the herd lumbers onto the banks to feed on grasses. Because of their size, adult hippos fear no predators, though their young must be closely guarded.

The most primitive of the primates are the lower primates, or prosimians, nearly all of which are nocturnal. Most are found on the island of Madagascar, where they developed in isolation from their monkey relatives; additional species live in Africa and Asia.

The leopard, *Panthera pardus*, emerges at dusk to ambush its prey. It favors the surprise attack, frequently springing down on its victim from a tree.

Wide-eyed lemurs, aye-ayes, lorises, and bushbabies all belong to the prosimian family. Generally small and secretive, they creep about through the treetops in search of insects and fruit. Africa's bushbabies are the most agile of this group, known for their ability to leap from tree to tree. The strangest is the aye-aye of Madagascar, whose incredibly long middle finger is used to extract insects from tree hollows. Until recently, the aye-aye was greatly feared by the natives, who believed that the slightest touch of this finger would result in death.

The higher primates are mostly diurnal. The exceptions are the howler monkey and the douroucouli, both of which live in tropical America. They have probably chosen a night-active lifestyle due to the crowded conditions of the jungle. These animals travel in bands and keep in touch with each other through loud vocalizations.

Only in recent centuries has humankind begun to adapt to life at night, and only with the aid of artificial lights that temporarily banish the darkness. Armed with new devices like radio collars and infrared lights, we are just beginning to probe and understand nature's nighttime world.

Above: The fruit bat, *Myotis myotis,* is also known as a flying fox. It makes no attempt to hide by day; predators are discouraged by its foul odor. *Left:* A mouse-eared bat hones in on a cricket on a stump. The bat locates its prey through echolocation. *Opposite:* Unlike insect-eating bats, fruit bats rely on their excellent night vision when navigating in the darkness. They feed on ripe fruit, which they find through their keen sense of smell.

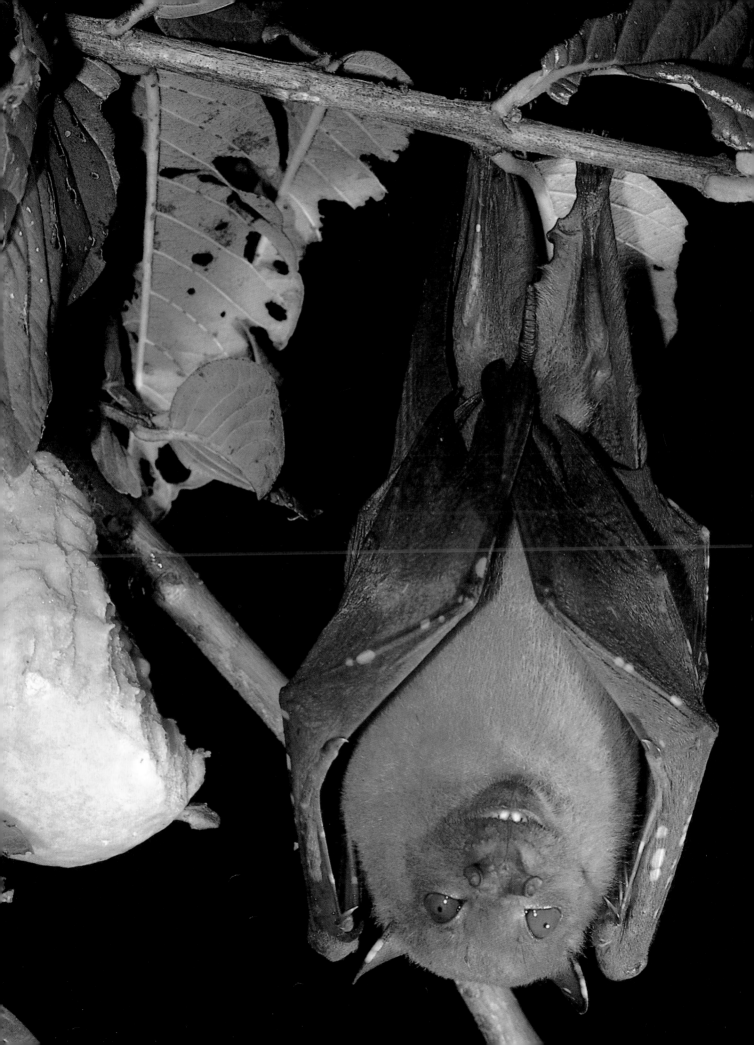

This page: A vampire bat, *Desmodus rotundus,* prepares to launch into the night in search of its warm-blooded prey. When it finds a sleeping animal, it makes an incision with its razor-sharp front teeth, then laps up the blood with its tongue. The groove on its lower lip is designed to let the liquid flow in. *Opposite:* A mouse falls victim to a pair of false vampire bats, *Megaderma cor.* These nocturnal carnivores also feed on frogs, lizards, birds, and other bats.

Above: A flying fox, or Indian fruit bat, rests on a tree branch. These large bats are found only in the tropics. *Opposite:* Fruit bats may travel up to 30 miles in search of a meal. By day they roost in large, tree-top colonies.

Index of Photography

TIB indicates The Image Bank